Learning to Read, Step by Step!

Ready to Read   **Preschool–Kindergarten**
• big type and easy words • rhyme and rhythm • picture clues
For children who know the alphabet and are eager to
begin reading.

Reading with Help   **Preschool–Grade 1**
• basic vocabulary • short sentences • simple stories
For children who recognize familiar words and sound out
new words with help.

Reading on Your Own   **Grades 1–3**
• engaging characters • easy-to-follow plots • popular topics
For children who are ready to read on their own.

Reading Paragraphs   **Grades 2–3**
• challenging vocabulary • short paragraphs • exciting stories
For newly independent readers who read simple sentences
with confidence.

Ready for Chapters   **Grades 2–4**
• chapters • longer paragraphs • full-color art
For children who want to take the plunge into chapter books
but still like colorful pictures.

STEP INTO READING® is designed to give every child a successful
reading experience. The grade levels are only guides; children will progress
through the steps at their own speed, developing confidence in their reading.
The F&P Text Level on the back cover serves as another tool to help you
choose the right book for your child.

Remember, a lifetime love of reading starts with a single step!

The publisher wishes to thank Michael K. Weisberg
of the American Museum of Natural History
for reading this manuscript for accuracy.

Text copyright © 1987 by Edith Kunhardt.
Cover and interior illustrations copyright © 1987 by Michael Eagle.
All rights reserved. Published in the United States by Random House Children's Books, a division
of Random House LLC, a Penguin Random House Company, New York.

Step into Reading, Random House, and the Random House colophon are registered trademarks of
Random House LLC.

Visit us on the Web!
StepIntoReading.com
randomhouse.com/kids

Educators and librarians, for a variety of teaching tools, visit us at
RHTeachersLibrarians.com

Library of Congress Cataloging-in-Publication Data
Kunhardt, Edith.
Pompeii . . . buried alive! / by Edith Kunhardt ; illustrated by Michael Eagle. p. cm. —
(Step into reading. Step 4 book) Summary: A simple retelling of the fateful days in 79 A.D. when
Mt. Vesuvius erupted and the people in the ancient town of Pompeii perished.
ISBN 978-0-394-88866-8 (trade) — ISBN 978-0-394-98866-5 (lib. bdg.)
1. Pompeii (Extinct city)—Juvenile literature. 2. Vesuvius (Italy)—Eruption, 79—Juvenile
literature. [1. Pompeii (Extinct city). 2. Vesuvius (Italy)—Eruption, 79.] I. Eagle, Michael, ill.
II. Title. III. Series. DG70.P7 K86 2003 937'.7—dc21 2002013645

Printed in the United States of America   70 69 68 67 66 65

This book has been officially leveled by using the F&P Text Level Gradient™ Leveling System.

Random House Children's Books supports the First Amendment and celebrates the right to read.

POMPEII...
Buried Alive!

By Edith Kunhardt

Illustrated by Michael Eagle

Random House 🏠 New York

1

The Sleeping Giant

Once there was a town named Pompeii. Say: pom-PAY. Near the town there was a mountain named Vesuvius. Say: veh-SOO-vee-us.

The people in Pompeii liked living by the mountain. It was a good place to grow grapes. It was a good place to raise sheep. And—it looked so peaceful!

But the mountain was really a dangerous volcano. It was like a sleeping giant. If the giant woke up, it could destroy the town.

Did the people know about the danger? No, they did not!

A volcano is a special kind of mountain. It has a hole at the top.

One day—almost two thousand years ago—something was happening under Vesuvius.

Way down deep it was very, very hot. It was so hot that rock was melting. As the rock melted, a gas was made. The gas was trying to escape.

The gas and the melted rock were mixed together. The mixture was hot and bubbly. The gas was pushing the melted rock up through Vesuvius.

The melted rock was about to blast right out the hole at the top!

The day started out the way it always did. The sun rose. People began coming to Pompeii with things to sell.

Fishermen were bringing fish.

Peddlers were bringing melons and straw hats.

Farmers were bringing vegetables.
Shepherds were bringing sheep.
Carts rumbled through the narrow
gates and into town.

The noisy carts in the streets woke up the people in the houses. The family who lived in one of the biggest houses was soon busy.

The mother went to pray in the courtyard. She put flowers by the statue of a god.

The father began to dress. His slave helped him.

The children were playing. They were glad it was summer.

The slaves in the kitchen were making breakfast.

No one in the house knew that something terrible was going to happen.

After breakfast the children went outside. The streets were crowded. People were at work inside the shops.

Bakers were busy baking flat bread. Weavers were busy weaving wool cloth. Potters were busy making clay pots.

Slaves were getting water at a
fountain. A musician was playing
his flute.

No one in the street knew that
something terrible was going to happen.

By late morning many men were at the bathhouse. They were having a good time. Some men were playing ball. Some men were lifting weights. Some men were talking in the steam room. Others were soaking in the hot pools.

The father from the big house was
there. His slave was rubbing oil on
his back.

No one at the bathhouse knew that
something terrible was going to happen.

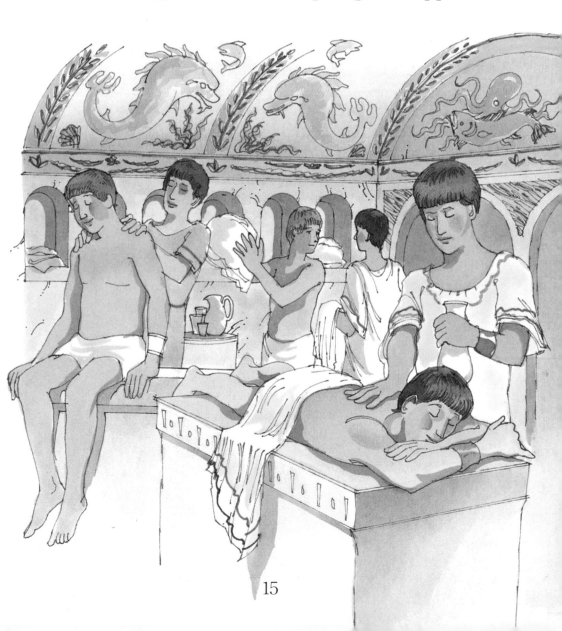

By noon the town meeting place was full of people.

Some people were looking for things to buy. Some people were talking to their friends. Lawmakers were meeting to make new laws. Visitors were looking at the beautiful buildings.

The mother from the big house was there. She was praying in the temple.

No one in the town meeting place knew that something terrible was going to happen.

2

The Giant Wakes Up

Suddenly the ground began to tremble. All of the houses in Pompeii began to shake. The giant was waking up!

Then there was an enormous cracking sound. The top of Vesuvius blew off! A huge cloud of dust and ash came pouring out!

Everyone began to scream.

People came out of their houses to look at the huge cloud. Shopkeepers came out of their shops.

Bakers forgot about their bread. Farmers forgot about their fruits and vegetables. And lawmakers forgot about the new laws.

The cloud was getting bigger and bigger.

The cloud hid the sun. It was dark. Tiny hot pebbles began to fall on the people in Pompeii.

Some people found pillows to cover their heads. Others hid inside their houses.

Everyone was running and pushing and shoving and shouting. Some people ran toward the town gates to get away. Others went home to protect their jewelry and gold coins.

A few went to the temple to pray. Could the gods save them?

23

The day became as dark as night. A horrible smell filled the air. It was like rotten eggs.

People rushed toward the sea. A few held torches to light the way.

The sea was wild. Huge waves kept crashing onto the beach. Fish were left flopping in the sand.

The family from the big house was able to get into a boat. They were able to get away.

When the pebbles fell on Pompeii,
many people could not escape. They
were trapped under the pebbles.

Then hot ashes began pouring out of
the volcano. The ashes fell on the people.
The ashes were hot enough to make hair
sizzle!

The people in the streets tried to protect themselves. They hid in corners and behind walls. They covered their faces with their hands and clothes.

But the ashes piled up higher and higher. The people could not move. The people could not breathe. They were trapped under the ashes.

The ashes kept falling!

Heaps of ashes filled the streets.
The ashes spilled into the houses.
They piled up to the first-story
windows. They piled up to the
second-story windows.

The people inside the houses were trapped too.

But Vesuvius was not done!

Now a great cloud of poisonous gas rushed out of the mountain. The cloud covered Pompeii.

A great river of hot ashes and gases raced down the side of the mountain. The river flowed right over the walls of the town.

No one in Pompeii was saved.

Across the bay a boy stood watching. His name was Pliny. Say: PLIN-ee.

Pliny saw the strange cloud that came out of Vesuvius. He saw the darkness over Pompeii. Later he heard about the hot ashes and pebbles and the wild sea.

Did Pliny ever forget that day? No, he did not!

3

Buried Alive!

The ashes fell on Pompeii for two days. Then it was over. The huge cloud was gone. The mountain was quiet.

The ashes cooled and became hard. Only the tops of buildings showed above them. The whole town had been buried alive!

Some of the people who had left in
boats came back. They came to look for
their houses. They came to look for their
belongings. They came to look for their
friends.

But everything was sealed under
the ashes.

Pliny grew up. He became a writer.
He wrote about the huge cloud that came
out of Vesuvius. He wrote about the
volcano that buried Pompeii.

Many years went by. Vesuvius erupted again and again. More ashes fell on the town. At last there was no sign that anyone had ever lived there.

By and by, people forgot about the town named Pompeii.

Hundreds of years later the ashes on top changed into soil. Grass began to grow. People built houses right above the buried town.

They built a new town on top of Pompeii. They did not even know that the old town was there!

Then people began to read Pliny's
letters. They read about a buried town
named Pompeii.

Where was Pompeii? Nobody knew.

One day some workers were digging a
tunnel for water. They found pieces of an
old wall under the ground. But they did
not know that the wall was part of a
town.

Many years later more people came to dig in the same place. They found more buildings. Was there a town under the ground? Was it the town Pliny wrote about?

Then one of the diggers found a stone. It had a name carved on it. The name was POMPEII.

People were very excited. The lost
town of Pompeii was right there—under
their feet!

If they could uncover it, they could
see how people lived long ago.

Scientists began digging. They worked
slowly and carefully. They used many
tools. They brushed away the ashes.
They did not want to destroy anything.

The scientists found beautiful gold
bracelets. They found unbroken eggs.

They found pictures made of colored
stones. These pictures are called
mosaics. Say: mo-ZAY-iks.

And they found the people who had
died.

At first the scientists found only a few skeletons.

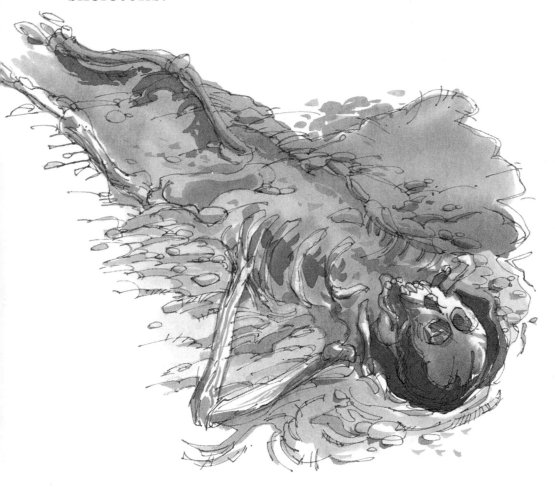

Then they saw strange holes in the hard ashes. They poured plaster into the holes. When the plaster dried, the plaster casts were shaped just like people!

The plaster casts showed how the
people looked when they died. There was
even a plaster cast of a dog on a chain.

Today the old town of Pompeii is like a great big museum without a roof.

Pompeii is in Italy. People come from many lands to visit. They want to see the shops and houses of long ago.

And they want to see Vesuvius, too. It is the most famous volcano in the world.

Scientists watch the volcano very carefully. How much gas is coming out of the ground? How hot are the rocks near the volcano? How much does the earth shake?

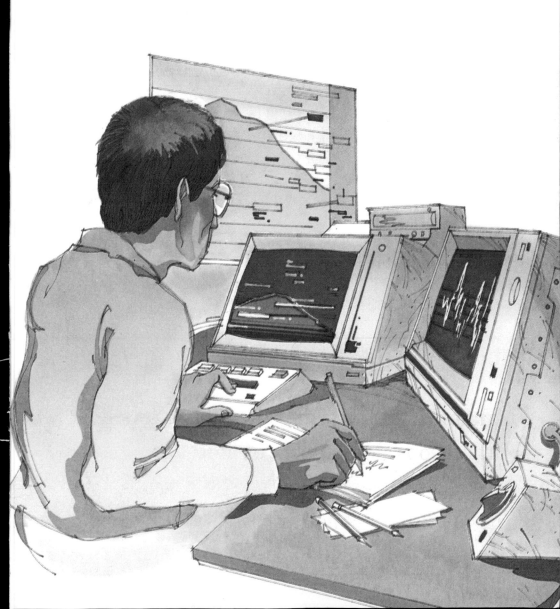

Look! A farmer is taking care of his grapevines. They grow on the side of the mountain named Vesuvius. Nearby a lizard is resting on a warm rock.

It is a peaceful day in Pompeii.

The giant is sleeping.

When will the giant wake up again? Nobody knows.